SCHWERIN

Im Spiegel der Seen
Lakeside Reflections

Bei Tag und bei Nacht dominiert der Dom das Straßenbild der Innenstadt wie hier in der Buschstraße, deren Verlauf einmal die Stadtgrenze am Wasser des Pfaffenteichs bildete.

The cathedral dominates the cityscape day and night - Buschstrasse, once the city's borderline, taking its course along the banks of Pfaffenteich.

SCHWERIN

Im Spiegel der Seen

Lakeside Reflections

SCHMIDT RÖMHILD
Verlagsgesellschaft mbH Schwerin

Herausgeber:
Norbert Beleke
Texte und Konzeption: Dietrich Barthel

Mit freundlicher Unterstützung durch die Stadtverwaltung
der Landeshauptstadt Schwerin

Fotos: Rainer Cordes;
Argus Luftaufnahmen Steffen Köppe (7): S. 11, 19 u., 29 (u. Umschlag-Rückseite), 34 o., 46 u., 65 u., 78u.;
Vor- und Nachsatz: Lothar Steiner;
S. 74/75: Staatliches Museum Schwerin

Übersetzung: St. Clair Consulting
Lektorat und Projektleitung: Thomas Sliepen
Grafische Gestaltung und Gesamtherstellung: Verlagsgruppe Beleke

2. überarbeitete und aktualisierte Auflage

Verlagsgruppe:
Verlag Beleke GmbH, Essen, Dortmund, Düsseldorf, Lübeck, Wiesbaden
NOBEL-Verlag GmbH, Essen – DAS RATHAUS Verlagsges. mbH Essen
SCHMIDT-RÖMHILD – Deutschlands ältestes Verlags- und Druckhaus seit 1579 –
Lübeck, Berlin, Essen, Wiesbaden
HANSISCHES VERLAGSKONTOR GmbH, Lübeck
SCHMIDT-RÖMHILD Verlagsgesellschaft mbH Leipzig, Rostock, Schwerin
ELVIKOM Film-Verlag GmbH, Essen
ntv neue television FILM-TV-PRODUKTION GMBH, Essen
Internet: www.beleke.de, www.schmidt-roemhild.de

ISBN 3-7950-4102-3

Die Markenzeichen Schwerins auf einen Blick: das überall gegenwärtige Wasser der Seen, das Schloss und die Staatskanzlei als Insignien der Landesmetropole, das Mecklenburgische Staatstheater und die Gemäldegalerie des Staatlichen Museums als Repräsentanten des Kulturpotenzials.

The unmistakable townscape of Schwerin - the chain of lakes, the Schloss, the State Chancellery, the insignia of the state capital, the Mecklenburgische Staatstheater and the picture gallery of the Staatliches Museum are evidence of the cultural diversity of the region.

Zwischen den Wassern der Seen verlaufen die Verkehrswege der Stadt. Auch dem Schienenstrang der Bahn gelingt es, die City zu erreichen.

The street system has been integrated into the complex pattern of the lakes. Even the railway somehow manages to wind its way into the city.

Schwerin im Spiegel der Seen

Schwerin – Lakeside Reflections

Der Dom und Köln, Semper und Dresden, die Strafpunkte und Flensburg, das Hofbräuhaus und München, die Wartburg und Eisenach, der FC und Kaiserslautern: Begriffe und Städte, die unzertrennliche Paare bilden und einander gedanklich zwingend ergänzen. Es bleibe dahingestellt, ob sol-

Cologne and the Dom; Dresden and the Semperoper; Flensburg and its index of German road traffic offenders; Munich and the Hofbräuhaus; Eisenach and the Wartburg; Kaiserslautern and FC Kaiserslautern football club. Things often come in pairs. Indeed, it would seem they are inextricably

che assoziierenden Stichworte der jeweiligen Stadt zum Vorteil oder zum Nachteil gereichen. Bei Flensburger Punkten dürfte das Urteil klar zu treffen sein, aber selbst der berühmte Dom kann allzu schnell andere Trümpfe auf der Habenseite des städtischen Imagebildes überdecken.

Mit solchen Imagepaaren kann und will Schwerin nicht dienen. Auch zuweilen geäußerte Vergleiche wie „Florenz oder Venedig des Nordens" oder auch „Binnenalster Schwerins" für den Pfaffenteich sind ähnlich weit hergeholt wie die

linked. Such links may be of a positive or negative nature - who is to say? In the case of Flensburg, of course, there can be little doubt; the central index acts as a constant reminder to all traffic offenders. But then again even the famous Dom in Cologne may prove a disadvantage. After all, it tends to overshadow many other treasures Cologne has to offer.

Schwerin is a city which does not wish to be labelled. Terms such as "Florence or Venice of the North" or even comparing the lake known as Pfaffenteich with Hamburg's Bin-

Schwerin erwacht. Aus dem Morgennebel erheben sich die Türme der Paulskirche, des Doms und der Schelfkirche.

Early morning in Schwerin. The towers of the Pauluskirche, the cathedral and Schelfkirche in the early morning mist.

Mecklenburger Schweiz, die nun alles andere als alpinen Charakter hat. Und trotzdem ist von allem etwas da. So ist es wohl eher das Mosaik der Vorzüge, das der Stadt so gut bekommt und das für Gäste wie Bewohner die besondere Attraktivität Schwerins erleben lässt.

Das Stadtbild Schwerins gibt es gleich zweimal. An allen Ecken spiegelt sich die Stadt in ihren Seen, die nach allen Himmelsrichtungen Schwerin umgeben und deren Ufer bis an die City reichen. Ein bisschen Venedig also schon. Aber Vergleiche hinken bekanntlich. Hier ist das Wasser gerade einmal dort - und auch noch unterirdisch - kanalisiert, wo es den Pfaffenteich mit dem Burgsee verbindet.

Dafür aber sind die Wasserflächen der zahlreichen Seen überall gegenwärtig. Die sich hartnäckig haltende Zahl von sieben Seen ist noch untertrieben. Zehn sind es bereits, wenn die ganz kleinen unberücksichtigt bleiben. Und der größte der Seen nimmt zugleich eine Spitzenposition unter den deutschen Gewässern ein. Sollen sich die Geister streiten, ob nun der Bodensee als deutsches und damit größtes deutsches Gewässer zählt. Platz vier ist dem Schweriner See auf jeden Fall gewiss. Über gut 22 Kilometer erstreckt er sich

nenalster are as far fetched as "Mecklenburger Schweiz" - after all there is absolutely no evidence of alpine features.

The truth is - Schwerin offers a little of everything. A rich mosaic of interesting sights, events and unspoiled areas of natural beauty makes the city attractive to the people of Schwerin and visitors alike.

For the visitor the city has a special surprise in store - Schwerin is situated amid a chain of lakes. The entire townscape is reflected on the shiny surface of the water, adding a touch of the magic of Venice. Maybe not a fair comparison. After all, Schwerin has only one canal and even it is underground, connecting the Pfaffenteich with the Burgsee.

The water of the lakes, however, is an omnipresent feature of Schwerin - the city is built around no fewer than seven lakes - in fact ten all in all - not counting the smaller ones. The largest of them is considered one of the most important lakes in Germany. We'll leave it to the water sprites to decide whether Lake Constance is wholly German and the largest lake in Germany and stick to the facts - the Schweriner See is definitely fourth on the list. It stretches more than 22 kilometres to the north, just a stone's throw away from Wismar

Das Herz der Stadt mit seinem Pfaffenteich.

The heart of the city with Pfaffenteich.

nach Norden, nur einen Katzensprung entfernt von Wismar und der Ostseeküste. Bis zu sechs Kilometern breitet er sich aus, durchtrennt vom Paulsdamm, der im 19. Jahrhundert auf einer natürlichen Bodenschwelle errichtet wurde, um das Wasserhindernis auf dem Verkehrsweg ins östliche Mecklenburg und nach Pommern zu überwinden. Das bewaldete östliche Steilufer gegenüber der Stadt ist nicht nur schöne Landschaftssilhouette, sondern eine geographische Besonderheit: Auf der eiszeitlichen Endmoränenschwelle verläuft die Wasserscheide zwischen der Ost- und der Nordsee. Zwar existiert mit dem Wallensteingraben eine alte künstliche und auf ihre Schiffbarkeit immer noch wartende Wasserverbindung zur Ostsee, für die es nicht erst seit des berühmten Feldherrn Zeiten sondern bereits seit dem 15. Jahrhundert Pläne und Unternehmungen gibt, über den Schweriner See die Verbindung zwischen Elbe und Ostsee herzustellen. Aber der natürliche Abfluss geschieht nach Süden über den Umweg der Elde und Elbe in die Nordsee, während die nahe Warnow durch den 12 Meter tiefer gelegenen Pinnower See bei Warnemünde die Ostsee erreicht.

Wer Schwerin kennen lernen will, ist gut beraten, mit einem Blick aus der Vogelperspektive zu beginnen. Gelegenheit gibt es reichlich: dem besteigbaren Domturm zu Füßen die engen Straßen und Gassen der Altstadt, der Markt und, wenn sich der Blick erhebt, die Weite des Schweriner Sees, die Seenkette, die Wälder. Oder der Blick vom Fernsehturm über die ganze Stadtlandschaft mit ihren vielen blauen und grünen Flächen, dem Dom und dem Schloss und bei guter Sicht über den großen See bis zu den Türmen der Hafenstadt Wismar.

Und natürlich der vom benachbarten Petersberg gestartete Rundflug , wie viele Aufnahmen dieses Buches eindrucksvoll belegen.

Ihren besonderen Reiz hat die Schweriner Landschaft der Weichseleiszeit zu verdanken, nach deren Rückzug der hügelige Endmoränenzug mit seinen großen Findlingen und seinen Söllen zurückblieb. Der bunte Wechsel von malerischen Seen, sanften Hügelketten und Talmulden, mit Wäldern, Wiesen und Wasserläufen ist das attraktive Ergebnis der Gletscherzungen und Schmelzwässer aus dieser Zeit.

Wasser und Wald stehen in vielen Gebieten Schwerins im unmittelbaren Dialog. Grün sind die südlichen Uferzonen des Schweriner Sees, die in den Parkanlagen des Schlosses beginnen und nahtlos übergehen in die Waldgebiete bis zu den Steilhängen des Görslower Ufers im Osten. Auch die Wälder auf der Halbinsel Schelfwerder, an den Ufern des Neumühler Sees und auf der Insel Kaninchenwerder mit ihrem Aussichtsturm auf dem Jesarberg laden bereits im Stadtgebiet zum Wandern ein.

and the shores of the Baltic Sea and has a width of 6 kilometres, interrupted by the Paulsdamm, built on a natural shelf during the 19th century in order to overcome the obstruction and leading to the eastern part of Mecklenburg and Pomerania. The steep wooded bank in the east, facing the city, does not just create a beautiful silhouette, it is also a unique geographical feature. The water-shed between the Baltic Sea and the North Sea runs along a terminal moraine shelf, created during the Ice Age. The Wallensteingraben is an artificial connection between the River Elbe and the Baltic Sea via Schweriner See, based on plans and projects dating back to the 15th century - well before the time of the famous Field Marshal. It is still waiting to be utilized. The natural flow of the water running into the North Sea takes its course towards the south, making a detour via the Rivers Elde and Elbe, whilst the River Warne meets the Baltic Sea near Warnemünde having made its way through Pinnower See, which is situated 12 kilometres below the river.

Those who want to get a full impression of Schwerin should take a bird's-eye-view. There are many possibilities for such a venture - the tower of the cathedral for one, looking down on the narrow streets and lanes of the old part of Schwerin and the market square; in the distance the waters of the Schweriner See, the chain of lakes and further beyond the woods. A view from the television tower includes the entire cityscape with its criss-cross pattern of blue and green, the cathedral and the Schloss and on a clear day across the great lake, the towers of the port of Wismar. And there is of course the possibility of the sightseeing flight, starting from the neighbouring Petersberg, as the many impressive photographs in this book will show.

The many areas of great natural beauty around Schwerin were created during the third and last Ice Age in northern Germany, leaving behind a hilly terminal moraine ridge with a number of large boulders and indentations. The colourful pattern created by picturesque lakes, gentle foothills and valleys, fringed by woods, meadows and brooks is an attractive heritage, a result of glacial deposits and melted ice.

In many areas surrounding Schwerin water and trees merge without any form of transition. The southern slopes of the Schweriner See are green - they start in the park of the Schloss and are immediately followed by wooded areas extending right up to the steep slopes of the Görslow shores in the east. The woods on Schelfwerde peninsula, along the banks of Neumühler See and the island of Kaninchenwerder with its lookout tower on the Jesarberg is particularly inviting, the ideal place for a long walk.

This unique combination of city- and waterscape will be utilized when it comes to creating an image of "Schwerin im

Diese einmalige Verbindung von Stadt- und Wasserlandschaft, Schwerin also im Spiegel der Seen, wird auch die Bundesgartenschau prägen, die für das Jahr 2009 vorbereitet wird.

In ihrer langen Geschichte - Schwerin ist die älteste Stadt des Landes und nach Lübeck die zweitälteste Deutschlands östlich der Elbe überhaupt - entstand in dieser Naturlandschaft aus einer kleinen slawischen Siedlung eine faszinierende Stadtlandschaft. Sicherlich hatte Heinrich der Löwe nicht so sehr die Reize landschaftlicher Schönheit im Sinn sondern eher politische und strategische Ziele, als er den Kampf gegen die ansässigen slawischen Obotriten unter ihrem Fürsten Niklot wagte. Der Schweriner See sorgte für den natürlichen Schutz der Inselburg nach Osten. Nun sollte es eine neue Stadt auch nach Westen tun. Nach dem Sieg über Niklot ließ Heinrich die zerstörte Burg Zuarin (slawisch für tierreiche Gegend) als deutschen Grafensitz wiedererrichten. In ihrem Vorfeld gründete er 1160 die Stadt Schwerin und holte das Bistum hierher aus dem heutigen Dorf Mecklenburg, das dem ganzen Land den Namen gab.

Das Land aber blieb als Lehen in den Händen von Niklots Söhnen. So sicherte sich Heinrich den Rücken im eroberten

Spiegel der Seen" - is an integral part of the plans for the National Flower Show, to be opened in 2009.

During its long history - Schwerin is the oldest town in the state after Lübeck, and the second oldest in Germany east of the River Elbe - the city grew from a small Slavonic settlement into a fascinating townscape. Henry the Lion, however, will hardly have chosen the site because of its natural beauty, but rather for political and strategic reasons, when battling against the Slavonic tribe of the Obotrites under their leader Prince Niklot. Schweriner See gave natural protection to the island fortification towards the east. The new town was to offer protection against attacks from the west. After his victory over Niklot, Henry had the castle of Zuarin (Slavonic name for "land rich in animals"), which had been destroyed, re-built and made it the seat of his German earldom. In 1160 he founded the town of Schwerin and transferred the diocese from the village of Mecklenburg to the town. The state was named after the village of Mecklenburg.

The land remained in the hands of the sons of Niklot. For Henry this was politically expedient and guaranteed protection in a land he had taken by force. Two centuries later, the descendants of the Obotrites bought back the earldom.

Schwerin spiegelt sich im Wasser der Seen. Diesen Eindruck erlebt der Bahnreisende bereits eine Fußminute vom Hauptbahnhof entfernt auf seinem kurzen Weg zur City.
Im wahrsten Sinne des Wortes Höhepunkte im Stadtbild sind die Backsteinbauten des gotischen Doms …

Schwerin reflected in the waters of the lakes. An impression gained by the visitor almost immediately after having left the main railway station on the short walk into the city.
True highlights in the city skyline: the brick building of the Gothic Dom …

... und der barocken Schelfkirche.
Der Turmhelm von St. Nikolai über dem Ostufer des Pfaffenteichs kündet von der Schelfstadt , deren Grundriss am Beginn des 18. Jahrhundert gelegt wurde und deren barocke Stadtanlage als städtebauliches Kleinod besondere planerische Aufmerksamkeit genießt.

... and the Baroque Schelfkirche.
The helm roof of St. Nikolai towering above the eastern shores of Pfaffenteich bears witness to Schelfstadt - the ground plan was established at the beginning of the 18th century. The Baroque town is a true jewel where urban development is concerned. Town planning has also been given a lot of attention.

Erst seit einem Jahrhundert spiegelt sich der Domturm im Wasser des Pfaffenteichs, als er über das hohe Dach des gotischen Baus zur stattlichen Höhe von 117 Metern wuchs.

A century ago the cathedral tower was extended beyond the roof of the Gothic building to a proud 117 metres – it is reflected by the water of Pfaffenteich.

Land. Zwei Jahrhunderte später kauften die Nachfahren der Obotriten sogar die Grafschaft zurück. So kam es, dass das bis 1918 regierende mecklenburgische Herzogs- und später Großherzogsgeschlecht ihren Stammvater im slawischen Fürsten Niklot sah, der heute im Hauptportal des Schweriner Schlosses der Stadt entgegen reitet.

Der andere Reiter jedoch ist Heinrich der Löwe selbst, verewigt im noch heute gültigen Stadtwappen und als goldene Skulptur auf den Zinnen des Rathauses reitend. Sein Beiname ist als Denkmal gleich zweimal gegenwärtig. Auf dem Markt hat der Konstanzer Bildhauer Peter Lenk seine Version von dem erobernden Rivalen Barbarossas in Zement gegossen. An der Nordwestseite des gegenüberliegenden Doms steht wie auch vor den anderen Domstiftungen Hein-

Therefore the ruling dynasty of the House of Mecklenburg, in power up to 1918, looked upon the Slavonic Prince Niklot as their progenitor. His sculpture can be found in Schweriner Schloss in the main entrance, where, mounted on a horse, he rides towards the city. The second horseman is Henry the Lion, still part of the municipal coat of arms; the gilded sculpture has been placed high on the roof of the town hall. A second sculpture of Henry, rival to Frederick I (Barbarossa), by the artist Peter Lenk from Constance can be found in the market place. The sculpture has been cast in cement. At the north western part of the cathedral, situated opposite the market square, the sculpture of a lion can be found. Henry gave order to place statues of lions outside all cathedrals founded by him. The lion of Schwerin was the first free-

Vom Schloss reichte der historische Kern Schwerins bis zum Pfaffenteich, der einst Wehr- und Nährfunktion erfüllte. Seine aufgestaute Wasserfläche diente dem Schutz der Stadt vor feindlichen Angriffen, seine Wasserkraft dem Betreiben einer Kornmühle an der heutigen Mecklenburgstraße in Höhe Schloßstraße zur Versorgung der Bürger.

The historical part of Schwerin stretched from the castle right up to Pfaffenteich, which once acted as a means of fortification and as a water supply. The waters of the lake were dammed and provided protection against enemy attacks. The water was also utilized to operate a grain mill near Mecklenburgstraße on level with Schloßstraße, for the purpose of supplying the people of Schwerin.

richs die von ihm selbst in Auftrag gegebene Löwenplastik, die als erste freistehende Plastik nördlich der Alpen in die Kunstgeschichte einging.

Grafschaft und Bistum – zwischen der weltlichen und der geistlichen Machtzentrale musste sich Schwerin auf dem kleinen Stadthügel behaupten, bedrängt von Burg und Dom. Aber die Stadt profitierte auch davon. Der Dom als Wallfahrtsstätte zum angeblich in einem Jaspis eingeschlossenen Blutstropfen Christi brachte Pilgerströme und damit Einkünfte in die Stadt. Und die herzogliche Macht auf der

Zu Füßen des Doms das Wohnhaus des Schinkelschülers Georg Adolph Demmler, des Stadtplaners, des Architekten vieler Schweriner Repräsentationsbauten und des Baumeisters beim Schlossumbau.

Below the cathedral, the residence of Georg Adolph Demmler, pupil of Schinkel, town planner, architect and builder of many official buildings in Schwerin. He was also responsible for the rebuilding of the Schloss.

sich zum Schloss mausernden Burg verhalf Schwerin unter Renaissance-Herzog Albrecht zu einer Blütezeit, auf der die Stadt ihr Potenzial an Kunst, Bildung und Architektur aufbaute.

So liegt die Wiege der Schweriner Kulturlandschaft in der Blütezeit ihrer Residenzgeschichte, die die Renaissance auch Schwerin bescherte.

Noch heute existieren Zeugen einer Schweriner Zeit, die unter Albrecht ein nordisches Florenz gestalten wollte: das Schloss, das im 16. Jahrhundert die mittelalterliche Burg ablöste und noch heute zur Seeseite Renaissance-Fassaden trägt, die Mecklenburgische Staatskapelle, die mit ihrer Herkunft als ehemalige Hofkapelle zu den ältesten deutschen Orchestern zählt, die von Albrecht für die städtische Jugend gegründete schulgeldfreie Fürstenschule, das heutige Gymnasium Fridericianum.

Palastarchitektur, Kunstschätze, Theater, Musik haben seitdem die markanten Punkte in der Architektur und im Kulturleben Schwerins gesetzt.

Da ist das großherzogliche Schloss auf der stadtnahen Insel im Schweriner See in seiner einmaligen Verbindung von Architektur und Landschaft. Seine bescheidene Burgherkunft verleugnen heute prächtige vielgestaltige und vor allem viel betürmte Fassaden, die ältesten im Terrakotta-Schmuck des Lübecker Tonbildhauers Statius von Düren, die meisten in der Nachempfindung des Loire-Schlosses von Chambord. Dafür hat der Hofbaumeister und Schinkelschüler Georg Adolph Demmler gesorgt, der in der Mitte des 19. Jh. den großherzoglichen Auftrag erhielt zum generellen Umbau des herunter gekommenen Schlosses. Auch Dresdens Baumeister Gottfried Semper hat seine Ideen zur Neugestaltung beigetragen.

Heute ist das Schloss sowohl schönster Arbeitssitz eines deutschen Landtages, wie der damalige Bundespräsident Richard von Weizsäcker bei seinem Besuch der mecklenburgisch-vorpommerschen Volksvertretung feststellte, als auch der museale Touristen-Magnet schlechthin durch die faszinierende Kopplung von Architektur und Seenlandschaft und als Stätte glanzvoller Interieurs und Kostbarkeiten. Die Repräsentations- und Wohnräume der großherzoglichen Familie in der Fest- und in der Beletage mit dem Blick auf die Weite des Schweriner Sees sind nach umfangreicher Sanierung wieder der Öffentlichkeit zugänglich.

Aber Architektur des Schlosses beginnt nicht erst an der Baufassade. Der Rundgang auf der Schlossinsel lässt die meisterhafte Gartenbaukunst von Peter Joseph Lenné erleben mit seinem exotischen Baumbestand und seinen zwei Ebenen, die in der einzigartigen Uferlage miteinander kommunizieren. Besonderes Schmuckstück ist die Orangerie, die

standing sculpture known in the region north of the Alps at the time.

Earldom and diocese – ruled by a secular and an ecclesiastical overlord – Schwerin was hard pushed by castle and cathedral. But the town also benefited from this seemingly difficult position. The cathedral had become a place of pilgrimage, visited by vast numbers of Christians who came to see a jasper (or bloodstone) which was said to hold a drop of the Blood of Christ. And the Pilgrims, of course, spent money. The former castle slowly took on the characteristics of a palace and Count Albrecht - a true prince of the Renaissance - brought art, education and architecture to the town. Thus, Schwerin became a true cultural centre of the Renaissance.

Albrecht, who wanted to make Schwerin into a "Florence of the North" created many buildings which have survived to this very day - the Schloss which replaced the medieval castle during the 16th century, still shows a façade dating back to the Renaissance; so does the Mecklenburgische Staatskapelle, once home of the royal orchestra and oldest orchestra in Germany, as well as the Fridericianum, founded by Albrecht as a school, where the young of the town of Schwerin did not have to pay school fees.

Architecture, art treasures, the theatre and music came into their own during the Renaissance period.

A perfect example - where architecture and landscape merge in perfect harmony - is the grand ducal palace built on the island in Schweriner See. Its humble beginnings as a fortified castle have been all but obliterated. It has been enhanced by a façade with a rich array of towers, the oldest of which has been adorned with sculptures worked in terra cotta by the artist Statius von Düren, following the style of the Loire castle of Chambord. The plans for such rich decorations stem from the royal builder and pupil of Schinkel, Georg Adolph Demmler, who was put in charge by the Grand Duke to restore and rebuild the somewhat dilapidated palace during the middle of the 19th century. The builder Gottfried Semper also contributed to the plans.

Today the Schloss is probably the most beautiful state parliament seat in Germany, as acknowledged by the former President Richard von Weizsäcker during his first visit to the new state of Mecklenburg-Lower Pomerania. Its beauty attracts many tourists, interested in the stunning architecture merged with a landscape dominated by lakes. It also holds many exquisite treasures which are worth seeing. The former living quarters and the chambers and halls used for official visitors to the Grand Duke and his family, including the ground floor with a beautiful view of Schweriner See, have been restored and are open to the public.

Der Pfaffenteichkreuzer verkürzt die Wege und bietet interessante Blicke über die Stadt.

A shortcut across the water and beautiful views – the Pfaffenteich cruiser.

wie die gesamte Parkanlage nach Originalplänen und aufwendiger Restaurierung im ursprünglichen Glanz erstrahlt. Eine aus riesigen heimischen Findlingen errichtete Grotte erinnert an die Romantiksehnsucht des großherzoglichen Bauherrn. Ganz anders der Eindruck vom Schlossgarten, durch eine historische Drehbrücke mit der Schlossinsel verbunden. Hier hat Barock für geometrische Exaktheit und Proportionen gesorgt. Die Hauptachse bildet der Kreuzkanal mit Permoser-Plastiken. Zutaten lieferten die Jahrhunderte: auf hohem Sockel wieder ein Reiter, dieses Mal Friedrich Franz II. als Bauherr des Schlossumbaus, Laubengänge, ein Pavillon, der Englische Garten. Und schließlich geht der prächtige Park über in die bewaldete Uferzone des Schweriner Sees bis zur neugestalteten Strandpromenade von Zippendorf, zur Mueßer Bucht mit ihrem bäuerlichen Volkskundemuseum und weiter bis zum östlichen bewaldeten Steilufer bei Raben Steinfeld.

Doch zurück zum Schloss und weiter zur Stadt. Nur durch die Burgseebrücke vom weiträumigen Alten Garten getrennt, bildet das Schloss mit Staatskanzlei, Staatstheater und Staatlichem Museum ein repräsentatives Gebäudeensemble von beeindruckender Geschlossenheit, die deren Zusammengehörigkeit anschaulich belegt: Die exponierte Stellung als Landesmetropole hat schließlich wesentlich die kulturelle Landschaft befördert, die sich hier an der weiträumigen Platzanlage vor der Kulisse des Schweriner Sees und zwischen Regierungs- und Großherzogssitz mit Gemäldesammlung, Theater und Konzert präsentiert.

Vielleicht ist das heutige Theatergebäude eine Verbeugung vor der kulturellen Blütezeit der Renaissance auch in Schwerin und damit doch ein weiterer Beleg für das nordischen Florenz. Jedenfalls ist seine Architektur eng angelehnt an Formen der italienischen Hochrenaissance. Nach Entwürfen des Hofbaurates Georg Daniel wurde es 1886 anstelle eines Theaterbaus errichtet, der vom Schlossbaumeister Demmler ein halbes Jahrhundert zuvor gebaut wurde und schließlich einem Brand zum Opfer fiel. Der gleiche Demmler hat als sein erstes Werk auch das am Platz gelegene Gebäude der Staatskanzlei geschaffen. Viele weitere repräsentative Bauten wie Marstall, Arsenal und Rathausfassade stammen ebenfalls von ihm, aber noch bedeutsamer ist sein „Erweiterungs- und Verschönerungsplan" für die stadtplanerische Entwicklung der Stadt, dessen Konzept noch heute Handlungsansätze zur Stadtgestaltung bietet.

Von der frühen Geburtsstunde der Mecklenburgischen Staatskapelle war bereits die Rede. Wie sie hatte auch das Mecklenburgische Staatstheater seine erste Adresse am herzoglichen Hof. Lessings Freund und Mitstreiter Conrad Ekhof, bekannt als Vater der deutschen Schauspielkunst, gründete hier 1753 die erste deutsche Schauspielakademie, mit

However, the skills of architecture must go beyond the mere complex of buildings - when taking a walk on the island an incredibly beautiful vista of beauty presents itself to the visitor, created by the master of landscape gardening, Peter Joseph Lenné. The array of exotic trees and the two levels merge in perfect harmony, thus creating a unique picture as they wind their way along the shores of the lake. A true jewel in the crown is the Orangery. Together with the park, it has been painstakingly restored following original plans, resplendent in its old glory. A grotto created from vast boulders found in the area, is evidence of the romantic yearnings of the Grand Duke. A totally different picture has been created in the Schlossgarten, connected to the island by a swing turn bridge. Here, geometrical exactness is all pervasive - as was typical during the Baroque period. The main axis is formed by the cross canal, decorated with sculptures by Permoser. The pieces used were added across several centuries - placed on a high base, another horseman, this time Friedrich Franz II, who ordered the restoration of the palace, arbours, a pavilion and the Englische Garten. The splendidly landscaped park finally merges with the wooded banks of Schweriner See, leading all the way to the newly established promenade of Zippendorf, the Muesser Bucht with an open-air museum on rural folklore, and the wooded slopes in the east near Raben Steinfeld.

But back to the Schloss and on to the town. Divided from the generously laid-out square Alter Garten by the Burgseebrücke, the Schloss with the state chancellery, the state theatre and the state museum presents itself as an impressive complex of buildings providing a picture of perfect unity. As state capital Schwerin has been able to create a rich cultural landscape the main features of which are: Schweriner See, the royal seat and its art collection, theatre and concert hall.

It may well be that the building which houses the theatre can be seen as an example of the very best the Renaissance had to offer to a town like Schwerin - "Florence of the North" after all? Whatever the case may be, its architecture is an example of Italian High Renaissance at its best. It was built following plans by the court builder Georg Daniel in 1886. The new building replaced the old theatre created by Demmler, builder by royal appointment, half a century early, after it had been burnt to the ground. Demmler also created the building which houses the state chancellery - it was his first project. Many more official buildings were to follow, such as the Royal Stables and the Arsenal; the façade of the town hall was also created following his design. Even more impressive is the heritage he has left to this very day - traces of town development and beautification.

der er dem stationären Theaterbetrieb den Weg ebnete. Das 19. Jahrhundert stand vor allem im Zeichen des Musiktheaters. Felix-Mendelssohn-Bartholdy leitete das erste Schweriner Musikfest, Friedrich von Flotow führte das Haus als Intendant, Richard Wagners Opern wurden schon seit 1852 regelmäßig inszeniert für einen Besucherkreis bis Hamburg und Berlin. Das 20. Jahrhundert sah Dirigenten wie Kurt Masur, Heinz Fricke, Rudolf Neuhaus, Hartmut Haenchen als musikalische Leiter in Schwerin. Im Schauspieltheater knüpfte Lucie Höflich an die Ekhofsche Idee mit der Bildung einer neuen Schauspielschule nach dem 2. Weltkrieg an. Heute gehört das Mecklenburgische Staatstheater zu den großen leistungsfähigen Häusern in Deutschland, das mit großen Opern bei den Schlossfestspielen und Schauspielinszenierungen im Domhof den freien Himmel und den Sommer in die Spielzeit aufgenommen hat, zur Freude der Touristen und der Theaterfreunde vor allem aus dem norddeutschen Raum.

The history of the Mecklenburgische Staatskapelle was already given a mention earlier on. Both, the orchestra and the theatre were created by royal order. Conrad Ekhof, who was a friend of Lessing, and known as the father of German theatre and the founder of the first drama school to be established in Schwerin in 1753, paved the way for a permanent theatre. The 19th century was dominated by music drama. Felix Mendelsohn-Bartholdy conducted the first festival of music in Schwerin and Friedrich von Flotow acted as director. Since 1852, Wagner's operas were performed regularly for visitors who came from as far as Hamburg and Berlin. During the 20th century, musical conductors such as Kurt Masur, Heinz Fricke, Rudolf Neuhaus and Hartmut Haenchen worked in Schwerin. Lucie Höflich followed Ekhof's idea and created a new drama school after the Second World War. Today, the Mecklenburgische Staatstheater is one of the most productive theatres in Germany. The programme offers an array of Grand Operas, performed "open air" in the Domhof. It does not pause during the summer - to the great delight of the tourists and theatre lovers mainly of the area, who vastly enjoy the theatre festival at the Schloss.

The immediate neighbour of this place of thespian prowess is the Staatliches Museum. Originally the site had been reserved for a new palace because

Der Schweriner See ist ein Eldorado für Wasserfahrzeuge und Wassersport jeder Art.

The Schweriner See is an El Dorado for boats and watersports of any kind.

Benachbart zur künstlerischen Darstellung die künstlerische Präsentation. Am Platz des heutigen Staatlichen Museums sollte eigentlich ein neues Palais errichtet werden, weil das verfallende Schloss einer nach dem Wiener Kongress großherzoglich gewordenen Residenz nicht mehr repräsentativ genug erschien. Der großherzogliche und romantisch veranlagte Nachfolger aber wollte es anders. Er überließ die bereits gelegten Fundamente ihrem Schicksal und dem späteren Museumsbau und beauftragte seinen Hofbaumeister Demmler mit dem Umbau des alten Inselschlosses.

Der Sammelleidenschaft von Herzog Christian II. Ludwig ist es zu verdanken, dass die Schweriner Gemäldegalerie am Alten Garten eine Kollektion holländischer Gemälde aus dem 17. Jahrhundert von einmaliger Geschlossenheit und Vielfalt besitzt, die in ihrem Umfang und ihrer Qualität den internationalen Ruf des Schweriner Kunstmuseums begründet. Über diesen bedeutenden Bestand an Werken des Goldenen Zeitalters niederländischer Kunst hinaus ist die Gemäldegalerie reich an weiteren Kunstschätzen von der deutschen

the Schloss was beginning to deteriorate and was no longer in keeping with the new status of Grand Duchy, a status gained as a result of the Congress of Vienna. However, the new Grand Duke was of a romantic nature and he had a rather different plan. He left the newly laid foundations to the museum which was to be built later and ordered his royal builder Demmler to rebuild the old castle on the island.

The Schweriner Gemäldegalerie at Alter Garten has benefited from the pronounced "collector's instinct" of Duke Christian II Ludwig, who was responsible for most of the acquisitions. The sheer size and quality have given the Schweriner Kunstmuseum its international reputation. Apart from the marvellous array of works illustrating the full diversity of art of seventeenth-century Holland, there are outstanding examples of early German paintings (Lucas Granach), German, French and English eighteenth-century paintings, as well as contemporary art, including compositions by Marcel Duchamps, purchased by the museum after a spectacular exhibition held in Schwerin.

Spätgotik und Renaissance (Lucas Cranach), deutscher, französischer und englischer Malerei vom 18. Jahrhundert bis zur Gegenwart und bis zur Schweriner Sammlung von Werken Marcel Duchamps, die das Museum nach einer spektakulären Ausstellung aufkaufte.

Schwerins Stadtbild ist voller Kontraste: Repräsentationsbauten, die den Jahrhunderte alten Residenzcharakter der Stadt belegen, der gotische Backsteindom mit Relikten seines romanischen Vorgängers und wertvollem kunsthistorischem Inventar, bescheidene Bürgerhäuser, hier und dort noch im Fachwerk, vor allem in der Schelfstadt, die ihre kleingliedrige Struktur einer barocken Stadtanlage noch weitgehend erhalten hat, die Geschäftsstraßen schließlich als Stadtbild des 19.Jahrhunderts, als Schwerin die mittelalterlichen Grenzen überwand und sich nach Norden und Westen ausdehnte. Dort, wo heute die Hauptgeschäftsstraße, die Mecklenburgstraße verläuft, standen einst das Wasser des Pfaffenteichs und die Wehranlagen für Stadt und Schloss. Das 19. Jahrhundert begann, und hier sei wieder Schwerins Baumeister Demmler hervorgehoben, sich als Stadt am Wasser zu begreifen und diesen Vorzug als Chance für die weitere Stadtentwicklung zu nutzen.

The city of Schwerin has many faces - official buildings which bear witness to the city's status as a royal residence through several centuries, such as the cathedral following Gothic architecture built in brick, with traces of its Romanesque predecessor, as well as valuable art-historical fixtures, fittings and furniture, and somewhat more humble town houses, some of them half-timbered. Most of the town houses can be found in Schelfstadt which has very much kept its baroque character. The shopping area bears witness to changes made during the 19th century, after Schwerin finally grew beyond its borders established during the Middle Ages and expanded in the north and in the west. The main shopping street "Mecklenburgstrasse" was created in an area which was once part of the Pfaffenteich and the fortifications of the town and the Schloss. At the beginning of the 19th century, master builder Demmler envisaged Schwerin as a town built around water and saw this as the chance for further development.

Das Sportforum am Lambrechtsgrund ist Heimstatt des Schweriner Leistungssports und Olympiastützpunkt im Segeln, Boxen, Volleyball und in der Leichtathletik.

The sports centre at Lambrechtsgrund is home to competitive sport; it is the Olympic centre for sailing, boxing, volley ball and track-and-field athletics.

Diese städtebauliche Idee führen heutige Stadtplaner fort, wie nicht nur die neue Pfaffenteichtreppe als Bindeglied zwischen Wasser- und Stadtlandschaft belegt. Schwerin erlebte seit der Wiedervereinigung einen kräftigen Aufwind in der Innenstadt. Nicht von ungefähr hatte sie sich das Motto gesetzt „Schwerin setzt Segel". Und da ist nicht nur dem landschaftlichen Charakter Tribut gezollt. Noch nie hatte die Schweriner Innenstadt so viele Kräne und Bauzäune gesehen, die inzwischen den Eröffnungen wichen. Neue Geschäftszentren, die Gestaltung des Straßenraums und der Uferbereiche, ehrgeizige Verkehrsvorhaben zur Erschließung des Zentrums und zum Ausbau der Stadttangente sind eindrucksvolle Ergebnisse in der jüngsten Entwicklung Schwerins. Dafür hat Schwerin auch seinen Preis bekommen. An einem bundesdeutschen Wettbewerb zur attraktiven Stadtentwicklung hatten sich etwa einhundert ostdeutsche Städte beteiligt, und unter den acht ausgezeichneten war Schwerin.

This idea first put into practice by Demmler has remained the focal point of modern town planning. The new Pfaffenteichtreppe which connects water- and cityscape is a perfect example. Since reunification the city has been enjoying a new lease of life - the city is getting new impetus - the motto "Schwerin under full sail" is very fitting for this go-ahead place. Never before had the inner city of Schwerin seen quite as many cranes and building sites, with buildings springing up like mushrooms. New shopping centres, a reorganized street system including the embankment and ambitious plans of traffic engineering including the city centre and the extension of the ring-road, are impressive witnesses to the city's development during recent years. And Schwerin has already been given a first award - it came eighth in a German-wide competition of most attractive town development, in which approximately one hundred towns from the eastern states of Germany took part.

Das städtischste aller Schweriner Gewässer: der Pfaffenteich.

The lake known as Pfaffenteich bordered by the city.

Aufgestaut bereits zur Gründungszeit der Stadt, steht er noch heute unter der Mecklenburgstraße in Verbindung zum Burgsee (am oberen Bildrand). Bis zum 18. Jh. war die heutige Hauptgeschäftsstraße noch Wasserfläche bis weit in die City hinein. Ihr heutiger Name und ihre Richtung weist über den Pfaffenteich zum heutigen Dorf Mecklenburg, dessen Burganlage einmal dem ganzen Land seinen Namen gab.

Dammed up when the town was first founded, it is still connected with the Burgsee (upper edge of the picture) by a canal running under Mecklenburgstrasse. Up to the 18th century the present main shopping street was in fact lake. Its name was derived from the village of Mecklenburg, former fortification which the state has been named after.

Das Wohnhaus des Baumeisters Georg Adolph Demmler liegt unmittelbar am Pfaffenteich.

The residence of the famous master builder Georg Adolph Demmler is situated in the immediate vicinity of Pfaffenteich.

„Machen Sie die Nacht zum Tage in Schwerin" heißt es auf einem Schwerin-Plakat. Eine attraktive Beleuchtung schafft dafür beste Voraussetzung.

"Enjoy the nightlife of Schwerin" – a poster promoting Schwerin. Attractive lighting helps find the way.

Demmlerhaus und Arsenal am Pfaffenteich.

Demmlerhaus and Arsenal in close proximity to Pfaffenteich.

Kaufhaus Kressmann in der Mecklenburgstraße.

Kressman department store in Mecklenburgstrasse.

Im September trifft sich nicht nur Schwerin zum Altstadtfest rund um den Pfaffenteich.

In September, Schwerin plays host to many visitors to the Altstadtfest at Pfaffenteich.

Zu Füßen des großherzoglichen Klavierlehrers und Komponisten Friedrich Wilhelm Kücken, der eine Stiftung zur Unterbringung und Beköstigung junger Musiker gründete und sein Lied „Ach, wie ist´s möglich dann" der sangesfreudigen Nachwelt überließ, läßt es sich am Nordufer des Pfaffenteichs gut plaudern, essen und trinken.

Watched over by the grand ducal music teacher and composer Friedrich Wilhelm Kücken, who is the founder of an establishment where young musicians are accommodated, a couple of leisurely hours chatting, eating and drinking are most enjoyable. Kücken's song "How can it be ..." is still popular with those who love nostalgic music.

Das Schweriner FilmKunstFest feierte im Mai 2000 sein zehnjähriges Bestehen. Das größte Filmereignis der östlichen Bundesländer bezieht den öffentlichen Freiraum ein, wie hier die Ufertreppe des Pfaffenteichs.

In May 2000 the Schwerin FilmKunstFest celebrated its 10th anniversary. Many events of the largest film festival in the eastern part of Germany take place outdoors, for example on the steps leading to Pfaffenteich.

Kulturspektakel auf der Pfaffenteichtreppe sind fester Bestandteil im Veranstaltungskalender des Schweriner Kultursommers.

Cultural events staged on the steps of Pfaffenteich are part of the cultural summer scene in Schwerin.

Weihnachtsmarkt in der Mecklenburgstraße. Das Riesenrad am Pfaffenteichufer krönt im wahrsten Sinne des Wortes das vorweihnachtliche Treiben.

Christmas fair in Mecklenburgstrasse. The Ferris wheel at Pfaffenteich is a main feature at the fair.

Der Eingang zur städtischen Verwaltung im Stadthaus am Packhof.

Entrance to the administration offices in the city hall on Packhof.

Seit seiner Einweihung 1998 vereint das Stadthaus zum ersten Mal in Schwerins Stadtgeschichte die städtische Verwaltung unter einem Dach zwischen Hauptbahnhof und der unmittelbaren Innenstadt.
Vom Pfaffenteich ist der Ziegelsee durch einen Damm getrennt, der das Wasser des Aubaches wahrscheinlich schon zur Zeit der Stadtgründung zum Mühlenteich, dem heutigen Pfaffenteich, aufstaute.

For the first time since the official opening of the town hall in 1998, the city's administrative bodies are housed in one building, located between the main railway station and the city centre.
Pfaffenteich and Ziegelteich are divided by a dam. It is likely that it was built at the point of the foundation of the city, damming the water of Auerbach at Mühlenteich, later given the name Pfaffenteich.

Mit dem Arsenal am Pfaffenteich leitete Demmler den Weiterbau der Stadt nach Westen und Norden ein. Das Gebäude im Stil englischer Tudorgotik ist Sitz des Innenministeriums.

The Arsenal built on the banks of Pfaffenteich was the first building to be constructed following Demmler's plans of expansion to the west and the north. The style follows the architectural tastes of Tudor England and is the seat of the Ministry of the Interior.

Im alten Hafen künftig wohnen. Der ehemalige Binnenhafen hat seine ursprüngliche Bedeutung verloren. Er ist heute einer der Vorrangbereiche für den innerstädtischen Weiterbau der Stadt in attraktiver Nachbarschaft zum Wasser. - Vom alten Speicher zum Hotel.

The old harbour is to become a residential area. Once inland port, it has lost its former importance. It has become one of the foremost areas of inner-city expansion along the shoreline. Storehouses turned into hotels.

Seit 1998 präsentiert sich die Mecklenburgstraße in alter und neuer Schönheit. Nach aufwendiger Sanierung des unterirdischen Wasserkanals begann in der Mecklenburgstraße die Neugestaltung des innerstädtischen Straßenraums, die inzwischen das Straßenbild im gesamten Stadtkern bestimmt.

Since 1998, Mecklenburgstrasse has taken on a new face - resplendent features old and new. After the underground canal had been restored, the street system around Mecklenburgstrasse was reorganized, including the entire city centre.

In der Mecklenburgstraße.

Stroll along Mecklenburgstrasse.

FilmKunstFest
SCHWERIN
EINSICHTEN
KKH
PALL MALL
10-1

Geschäftshäuser in der Mecklenburgstraße.

Shops in Mecklenburgstrasse.

Das Postgebäude kennzeichnet die Mecklenburgstraße besonders eindrucksvoll als Boulevard des 19. Jahrhunderts. Auch die architektonische Verwandtschaft mit dem Johann-Albrecht-Stil mecklenburgischer Renaissance ist unverkennbar.

The Post Office buildings along Mecklenburgstrasse date back to the 19th century and add a touch of the "boulevard". The architecture follows the Johann-Albrecht-Stil of the Mecklenburg Renaissance.

Generalpostmeister und Ehrenbürger Heinrich von Stephan hatte wesentlichen Anteil am Bau der neuen Post.

The postmaster general and freeman Heinrich von Stephan played an important role in the building of the Post Office.

Beliebtes Fotomotiv: helles Fachwerk vor der mächtigen Backsteinfassade des gotischen Doms.

Popular motif for photographs - attractive half-timbered houses silhouetted against the vast brick façade of the Gothic cathedral.

Die Schmiedestraße verbindet den Markt mit der Mecklenburgstraße und führte einst zum Schmiedetor und aus der Stadt, bis die im Merian-Stich ersichtlichen Befestigungsanlagen die Zufahrt abschnitten.

Schmiedestrasse connects the market square with Mecklenburgstrasse. It used to lead towards Schmiedetor, out of the city up to the fortifications as seen in an engraving by Merian.

Schmiedestr.
Schweriner Kunstgewerbehaus

Die Marktbuchhandlung mit den Löwenbänken.

Bookshop at the Markt, with entrance flanked by lions.

Zum jährlich am Beginn des Sommers wiederkehrenden Töpfermarkt auf dem Schweriner Marktplatz bieten vor allem norddeutsche Keramiker ihre Waren feil.

Every year at the beginning of summer potters from the north of Germany show their wares at the Töpfermarkt at Schweriner Marktplatz.

Der Markt ist beliebter Auftrittsort für Kapellen und Musikanten. The market square is a popular spot for orchestras and musicians.

Hinter der einheitlichen Markt-Fassade des Rathauses versteckt sich eine bewegte Baugeschichte von der Gotik über die Renaissance bis zum Umbau durch Demmler im 19. Jh. Aufschlussreicher für die vielen Veränderungen des Rathausbaus ist die Ansicht vom Schlachtermarkt. Das gotische Durchgangsportal ist die älteste Hinterlassenschaft eines profanen Bauwerks in der Stadt.

The now uniform façade of the town hall hides an incredible history of structural changes, from the Gothic style and the Renaissance, to the period of rebuilding by Demmler during the 19th century. The view of the Schlachtermarkt makes the many changes the town hall underwent even more evident. The Gothic portal is the oldest legacy left of a secular building.

Der Dom begleitete die Stadt durch ihre lange Geschichte. Sein Vorgängerbau ist ebenso eine Stiftung Heinrich des Löwen wie die Dome von Lübeck und Ratzeburg auch. An den romanischen Vorgängerbau erinnert die erhalten gebliebene Paradiespforte an der Südseite. Die außergewöhnliche Länge des Kirchenschiffs von 100 Metern übertrifft die der großen hansischen Kirchen an der Ostseeküste.

The cathedral shares the long history of the town. Its predecessor was built by Henry the Lion, just like the cathedrals in Lübeck and Ratzeburg. The Paradiespforte, a portal at the southern part, acts as reminder of the old cathedral built in the Romanesque style. The unusual length of the nave of 100 metres makes it larger than any of the great Hanseatic churches along the Baltic coast.

Das Neue oder auch Säulengebäude zu Füßen des Doms am Markt diente einst als Markthalle. Nach Plänen des Schweriner Baumeisters Johann Joachim Busch entstand der klassizistische Bau mit dem barocken Mansardendach 1783 bis 1785. Im Jahr 1995 setzt der Konstanzer Bildhauer Peter Lenk seinen künstlerischen Kommentar zum Stadtgründer auf den Markt. Auf den Stelen gestaltet Lenk seine Sichten auf Episoden um Heinrich. Hier steht Barbarossas Widersacher dem Bildhauer Modell für den berühmten Braunschweiger Löwen.

The New Building or Building with Columns situated close to the cathedral in the market square was originally used as market halls. It was built from 1783 to 1785 following the plans of the architect of the Schwerin builder Johann Joachim Busch. The main building is classical, the roof is baroque. In 1995 Peter Lenk, a sculptor from Constance, created a column which is adorned with pictures depicting the life of Henry the Lion. The famous lion of Brunswick is dedicated to Henry, adversary of Barbarossa.

Der Löwe als Stadtgründer: Herzog Heinrich der Löwe gründete die Stadt. An seine Domstiftung erinnert die von ihm selbst in Auftrag gegebene Plastik, die erste freistehende nördlich der Alpen überhaupt.

The lion, symbol of the founder of the city – Duke Henry the Lion. The lion of Schwerin was the first free-standing sculpture known in the region north of the Alps at the time.

Nach 220 Stufen zum Rundgang des Domturms bietet sich ein einmaliger Blick auf die Stadt und ihre Seen.

It takes 220 steps up the cathedral tower to enjoy this unique view of the city and its lakes.

Ökumenischer Gottesdienst im Schweriner Dom. Die Ladegastorgel gehört zu den bedeutendsten Orgeln Europas aus der Zeit der Romanik. Der hölzerne Flügelaltar von 1495 mit dem Sandsteinrelief von 1420 gehört zu den kostbaren Kunstwerken im Dom.

Ecumenical church service in Schweriner Dom. The organ built by Friedrich Ladegast is considered to be among the most outstanding instruments in Europe, dating back to the Romantic period. The wooden winged altar, dating back to 1495, and the sandstone relief, created in 1420, belong to the most precious pieces of art in the cathedral.

Das Triumphkreuz von 1420 stammt aus der im 2. Weltkrieg zerstörten Marienkirche in Wismar.

The triumphal cross dates back to 1420 and comes from Marienkirche in Wismar, which was destroyed during the Second World War.

Die ehemaligen Stadthallen wurden nach dem 2. Weltkrieg ein Haus sowjetischer Offiziere und nun Bestandteil des „Schlosspark-Centers".

The former "Stadthallen" were used as an officers' mess for members of the Soviet army after the Second World War. They are now part of the "Schlosspark-Center".

Der Marienplatz als Schnittpunkt von Straßenbahnen und Bussen des Nahverkehrs ist am Ende des Jahrhunderts auch Geschäftszentrum geworden mit den Einkaufspassagen „Wurm", „Schlosspark-Center" und einem weiteren Handelshaus.

Marienplatz, an road intersection for busses and trams, became a popular shopping area at the turn of the century, with shopping malls such as "Wurm", "Schlosspark-Center" and others.

An die stadtgeschichtliche Vergangenheit als Spitze der Wehranlagen und Ausgangspunkt einstiger Ausfallstraßen erinnert am Marienplatz nichts mehr. Heute ist der Platz Nahverkehrsknoten der Stadt und Standort großer Einkaufspassagen

At Marienplatz little is left to serve as a reminder of the town's fortifications and its central position in the former network of arterial roads. Today the square has become a major hub for traffic and a location for large shopping malls.

Im Schlosspark-Center.

The Schlosspark-Center.

„Der Wurm" schlängelt sich als städtebaulich interessanter Passagenbereich durch ehemalige Hinterhöfe. Einkaufen, Begegnen und Erleben sind hier groß geschrieben.

The shopping centre "Der Wurm" winds its way through former backyards – shopping, chatting and having a good time made easy.

Schwerins Innenstadt ist zwar im wesentlichen vom 19. Jh. geprägt. Stadtbrände haben allzu oft und ausgiebig für die Zerstörung mittelalterlicher Bausubstanz gesorgt. Aber der Wechsel mit erhalten gebliebenem Fachwerk sorgt für besonderen städtebaulichen Reiz, wie hier in der Buschstraße.

The city centre was created almost entirely during the 19th century. Buildings dating back to the Middle Ages were destroyed during several major fires which raged through the town time and time again. The half-timbered houses which were saved from the fires add a charming touch to the city.

Der aufmerksame Stadtbummler wird nicht nur schöne Fachwerkfassaden sondern so manche interessante Details auch an jüngeren Häusern entdecken wie hier am „Tabakhaus" in der Friedrichstraße.

Walking through the city at leisure, the visitor will not only find beautiful half-timbered façades but also many modern houses with interesting architectural details, as in Friedrichstrasse ("Tobacco-house").

Die Schelfkirche St. Nikolai bildet den Mittelpunkt der barocken Schelfstadt, deren planmäßige Bebauung am Anfang des 18. Jh. begann.

Schelfkirche St. Nikolai is the centre of the Baroque Schelfstadt, constructed from the beginning of the 18th century onwards.

Die Schelfkirche aus dem frühen 18. Jahrhundert wurde von Jacob Reutz entworfen, der auch den Bebauungsplan für die „Neustadt auf der Schelfe" schuf. Die St. Nikolai gilt als bedeutendster sakraler Barockbau in Mecklenburg.

Schelfkirche St. Nicolai dates back to the beginning of the 18th century and was designed by Jacob Reute, who also created the plans for "Neustadt auf der Schelfe". St. Nikolai is the most significant religious Baroque building in Mecklenburg.

Das Schleswig-Holstein-Haus in der Schelfstadt als kulturelle Begegnungs- und Ausstellungsstätte ist nach aufwendiger Sanierung aus einem verfallenden alten Palais entstanden. Seinen heutigen Namen verdankt es der Initiative Schleswig-Holsteins in der Wendezeit, in den ehemaligen Bezirksstädten Mecklenburg-Vorpommerns die Sanierung von Gebäuden für gemeinsame kulturelle Projekte zu fördern.

Schleswig-Holstein-Haus has become a cultural meeting point. It was once a dilapidated manor house which has been restored. It was given its name following a restoration project run by the state of Schleswig-Holstein during the period of reunification, in order to promote cultural activities in former district towns of Mecklenburg-Vorpommern.

Die neue Plastik erinnert an den alten Schweinemarkt der Schelfstadt.

The new sculpture serves as a reminder of the old pig market of Schelfstadt.

Eckgiebel des Stammhauses der Sparkasse an der Schelfkirche.

Corner of the original Sparkasse building near Schelfkirche.

Das Ostufer des Pfaffenteichs wurde erst am Ende des 19. Jahrhunderts städtebaulich erschlossen und die Bebauung an das Wasser geführt wie hier in der Körnerstraße.

Towards the end of the 19th century the city's building was extended right up to the east bank of Pfaffenteich, as in Körnerstrasse.

„Obotriten, die Schlachtrösser rüstend" nennt der Berliner Bildhauer Christian Genschow seine Figurengruppen auf den Brückenpfeilern zum Schloss. Sie erinnern an den Feldzug Heinrich des Löwen gegen die unterlegenen Obotriten unter Niklot, dem Reiter in der Fassade des Schlossportals.

The sculptor Christian Genschow of Berlin has named his group of figures "Obotrites preparing their horses for battle". The figures have been placed on the pylons of the bridge leading to the Schloss. They are a reminder of the battle fought by Henry the Lion against the Slavonic tribe of the Obotrites under their leader Niklot, and their defeat. A sculpture of Niklot as a horseman has been integrated into the façade of the portal of the Schloss.

Im Hauptportal des Schlosses reitet Niklot, der slawische Obotritenfürst, der 1160 zwar von Heinrich dem Löwen geschlagen aber trotzdem zum Stammvater des mecklenburgischen Fürstengeschlechts wurde.

Niklot, ruler of the Slavonic tribe of the Obotrites was defeated by Henry the Lion in 1160, but nevertheless became the progenitor of the royal house of Mecklenburg.

Als Goldener Reiter ziert Heinrich der Löwe das Rathausdach. Schon seit der Stadtgründung trägt Schwerin das Siegel des Sachsenherzogs auch im Stadtwappen.

A gilded sculpture of Henry the Lion high on the roof of the town hall. The seal of the Saxon Duke has been part of the municipal coat of arms of Schwerin since the foundation of the town.

Im Burgsee spiegelt sich der Burgseeflügel des Schlosses, der 1913 völlig ausbrannte und heute den Plenarsaal des Landtages beherbergt.

The Burgsee wing of the Schloss is reflected in the waters of the Burgsee. It was completely burnt out in 1913 and is now used as the chamber of the Landtag.

Die goldene Kuppel über dem Hauptportal des Schlosses nach Entwürfen des Berliner Baumeisters Friedrich August Stüler wirkt wie die Krone großherzoglicher Macht schlechthin. Auf der Spitze steht Erzengel Michael mit dem Kreuz des Siegers über den Geist der Finsternis getreu dem Leitspruch des Schlossbauherrn Friedrich Franz II. „per aspera at astra" (durchs Dunkle zum Licht).

The gilded cupola above the main entrance of the Schloss was created following plans drawn up by Friedrich August Stüler. It is the very symbol of grand ducal power. At the top, the Archangel Michael bearing the cross of victory over the spirit of darkness, following the motto of Friedrich Franz II, who gave orders to build the Schloss, "per aspera at astra" (through darkness into light).

Hier schlägt das politische Herz des Landes. Der Plenarsaal des Landtages von Mecklenburg-Vorpommern und die Arbeitsräume der Abgeordneten liegen in unmittelbarer Nachbarschaft zu den großherzoglichen Repräsentationsetagen, die als Schlossmuseum der Öffentlichkeit zugänglich sind.

This is where the political heart of the state beats. The Chamber of the Landtag of Mecklenburg-Vorpommern and the offices of the elected representatives are situated in close proximity to the grand ducal official rooms, which are open to the public.

Der Burggarten bildet eine harmonische Einheit von Gartenbaukunst und Architektur. Zum wertvollen Baumbestand gehört die mächtige 140 Jahre alte hängende Rotbuche, die den Spazierweg mit ihren Zweigen überdacht.

The Burggarten is a fine example of 19th century landscape gardening. It features a vast tortured red beech tree which is 140 years old and provides a shady roof to visitors taking a stroll in the park.

Der großherzogliche Thronsaal nach Entwürfen des Berliner Architekten Friedrich August Stüler.

The throne room of the Grand Duke following plans of the architect Friedrich August Stüler.

Die herzogliche Ahnengalerie im Schweriner Schloss.

The ancestral portrait gallery in Schweriner Schloss.

Christian Ludwig krönt den Giebel des Gartenportals. Der Sammlerleidenschaft des Herzogs hat Schwerin den Grundstock seiner Kunstschätze von internationalem Rang zu verdanken.

A sculpture of Christian Ludwig has been integrated into the gable of the garden portal. The Duke was a great collector and he laid the foundation for Schwerin's collection of art treasures of international renown.

Eine der beiden Victoria-Statuen in der Orangerie.

One of two Victoria statues in the Orangery.

Nach aufwendiger Restaurierung ist die Orangerie wiederhergestellt.

Following a period of painstaking renovation, the Orangery has been restored to its former glory.

Der Kreuzkanal mit 14 Permoser-Statuen bildet die Hauptachse des Schlossgartens und weist auf den Schlossgartenflügel des Schlosses. Die barocke Parkanlage entwarf Jean Legeay wie damals üblich nach dem Vorbild des Parkes von Versailles.

The Kreuzkanal with its 14 sculptures by Permoser forms the main axis of the Schlossgarten, pointing towards the Schlossgarten wing of the Schloss. The park was laid out in the Baroque style by Jean Legeay, following the design of the park in Versailles, as was the fashion of the day.

Der Schweriner Fünf-Seen-Lauf wird an jedem ersten Juli-Sonnabend zum volkssportlichen Ereignis für über 2000 Lauf- und Wanderfreunde aus ganz Deutschland.

More than 2000 sports fans from all over Germany take part in the "Fünf-Seen-Lauf" (marathon along the shores of five lakes), staged on every first Saturday in July.

Liebesglück auf der Liebesinsel. Nur wenige Fußminuten vom Stadtzentrum entfernt lädt ein kleiner Ableger der Schlossinsel in landschaftliche Idylle ein …

Romance on Liebesinsel. Only a few minutes walk from the city centre, a small area of the main part of Schlossinsel is the ideal spot for an idyllic tête-à-tête …

... Und Kinderglück im Schlossgarten.

... And perfect for an outing – Schlossgarten.

Der Schlossgarten mit dem Kreuzkanal in seiner Hauptachse, den Laubengängen und dem Reiterstandbild Friedrich Franz II., des Bauherrn des Schlossumbaus.
An den barocken Schlossgarten schließt sich der Englische Garten an.

Schlossgarten with the main axis, the arbour and the sculpture of Friedrich Franz II, initiator of the rebuilding of the castle. The baroque Schlossgarten meanders into Englischer Garten.

Der Hafen der Weißen Flotte in der Schlossbucht am Alten Garten zwischen großherzoglichem Marstall (heute Sitz von zwei Ministerien) und dem Schweriner Schloss.

The harbour of the white fleet in the Schlossbucht at the Alter Garten located between the grand ducal stables (now seat of two ministries) and Schweriner Schloss.

Am Alten Garten in unmittelbarer Nachbarschaft von Schloss und Schweriner See präsentieren sich Mecklenburgisches Staatstheater und Gemäldegalerie des Staatlichen Museums.

The Mecklenburgische Staatstheater and the picture gallery of the Staatliches Museum are in the immediate vicinity of the Schloss and Schweriner See at the Alter Garten.

40 000 Jugendliche kommen alljährlich zum 1. Mai nach Schwerin zur Job-Parade, der größten Jugendaktion für Ausbildung und Arbeit in der Bundesrepublik.

Every year on May 1st, 40,000 young people come to Schwerin to visit the Job Parade, the largest event for training and work for young people in Germany.

Die Schlossfestspiele des Mecklenburgischen Staatstheaters gehören zu den größten europäischen Open-Air-Festivals und sind Höhepunkte des Schweriner Kultursommers. Als besonderes Ereignis erleben jährlich 40.000 Besucher Inszenierungen von Verdi- und Puccini-Opern wie hier bei „Ein Maskenball", „Rigoletto" und „Aida".

The Schlossfestspiele of the Mecklenburg State Theatre rank among the largest open air festivals in Europe and are the highlight of Schwerin's cultural event programme during the summer months. More than 40,000 visitors look forward to the delights of Verdi and Puccini operas, such as "Un Balla in Maschera", "Rigoletto" and "Aida".

Schloss und Schlossgarten werden Mittelpunkt der Bundesgartenschau 2009 sein.

Schloss and Schlossgarten will be part of the National Flower Show in 2009.

Zur Bundesgartenschau 2009 wird der Bereich vom Seglerhafen „Beutel" (links) über Schloss, Burgsee, Schlossgarten bis in die naturnahe Uferlandschaft des Schweriner Sees am Franzosenweg neu gestaltet bzw. rekonstruiert.

The area stretching from the sailing port "Beutel" (left) – via Schloss, Burgsee and Schlossgarten – to the shores of Schweriner See at Franzosenweg will be restructured for the 2009 National Flower Show.

Hochkarätige Kunst, von Cranach bis Polke, erwartet die Besucher im Staatlichen Museum Schwerin, direkt am Schweriner See gelegen. Mecklenburger Herzöge begründeten eine der umfangreichsten Sammlungen holländischer und flämischer Malerei des 16. und 17. Jahrhunderts in Europa.Viele große Namen des Goldenen Zeitalters sind vertreten, u.a. Fabritius, Rembrandt, Hals, Mieris, Steen, Brueghel und Rubens.

Outstanding works of art from Cranach to Polke await the visitor in the Staatliches Museum Schwerin, situated near Schweriner See. The counts of Mecklenbug collected many works of art by Dutch and Flemish painters of the 16th and 17th century. Many great names can be found, representing the Golden Age – Fabritius, Rembrandt, Hals, Mieris, Steen, Brueghel and Rubens.

Ernst Barlach,
Das Wiedersehen.
Mit der Stiftung 15 bedeutender Bronze-Plastiken des Bildhauers Ernst Barlach (1870-1938) durch den in Schwerin geborenen und heute in München lebenden Industriellen und Schweriner Ehrenbürger Ludwig Bölkow und seine Frau Eleonore Bölkow erfuhr die Skulpturensammlung des Staatlichen Museums Schwerin eine außerordentliche Bereicherung.

Ernst Barlach. Reunion. The industrialist Ludwig Bölkow, born in Schwerin and freeman of the city, and his wife Eleonore, now residents of Munich, contributed 15 sculptures by the artist Ernst Barlach (1870 - 1938) to the collection of the Staatliches Museum Schwerin.

Frans Hals d.Ä., Weintrinkender Knabe.
Schwerins Sammlung aus dem „Goldenen Zeitalter der holländischen Malerei" ist mit insgesamt 550 Gemälden die umfangreichste und geschlossenste in Deutschland. Namen wie Frans Hals d.Ä. mit zwei bezaubernden Knabenbildnissen, Rembrandt, Jan Lievens oder Ferdinand Bol stehen für die Porträtmalerei.

Frans Hals the Elder. Boy drinking wine. The Schwerin collection with 550 paintings from the Golden Age of Dutch Painting is the largest and most comprehensive in Germany. Artists such as Frans Hals the Elder (two beautiful portraits of young boys), Rembrandt, Jan Lievens or Ferdinand Bol are synonymous with portrait painting.

Holländische und flämische Malerei, wie hier in barocker Hängung, bilden zwar das Zentrum der Schweriner Kunstschätze , aber in Sonderausstellungen und mit Neuerwerbungen von Alexander von Jawlensky, Robert Delaunay, John Cage, Günter Uecker, Marcel Duchamp und Sigmar Polke stellt sich das Museum Tendenzen der Gegenwartskunst, um eine lebendige und vielschichtige Diskussion über deutsche und internationale künstlerische Positionen zu ermöglichen.

Although Dutch and Flemish painters, as depicted here in baroque frames, are the focal point of Schwerin's art treasures, the museum also showcases modern art, including artists such as Alexander von Jawlensky (new acquisitions), Robert Delaunay, John Cage, Günter Uecker, Marcel Duchamp and Sigmar Polke. The works are shown in a special exhibition, the objective being to promote in-depth debate throughout the national and international art scene.

Die Schleifmühle zwischen Schloßgarten und Faulem See ist als funktionstüchtige Wassermühle wiederhergestellt. In dem heutigen Museum wird interessierten Besuchern die historische Art des Steinschleifens vorgeführt, wie sie beim Umbau des Schlosses im 19.Jh. noch praktiziert wurde.

The Schleifmühle located between Schloßgarten and Fauler See is in full working order. The mill was used for grinding down stones following a method used through the centuries. Stones prepared by the mill were used for reconstructing the castle during the 19th century.

Auf einem alten slawischen Burgwall am Schweriner See wurde im Geiste der Ruinenromantik des 19. Jahrhunderts die Reppiner Burg errichtet.

Reppiner Burg was built on the site of an old Slavonic castle on Schweriner See following the romantic style popular during the 19th century.

Das für die mecklenburgische Dorflandschaft typische Niederdeutsche Hallenhaus des Freilichtmuseums wurde nach dem Dreißigjährigen Krieg gebaut und gehört zu den ältesten Bauernhäusern der Umgebung.

The open-air museum housed in a "hall", typical of the type of houses which dominate the landscape of Lower Germany. It was built following the Thirty Years' War and is one of the oldest farmhouses of the area.

Eine Dorflandschaft am See ist Museum geworden. Das Mecklenburgische Volkskundemuseum in der Mueßer Bucht mit seinem dörflichen Gebäudeensemble, seinem Inventar und seinen Veranstaltungen lädt ein zu einem Rundgang durch die bäuerliche Kultur der Arbeit, des Brauchtums und des Zusammenlebens.

A village on the shores of the lake made into an open-air museum. The Mecklenburgische Museum of Folklore located in Muesser Bucht invites visitors to experience culture, tradition and communal living as well as everyday chores in rural areas. The museum includes traditional buildings and inventory and also stages special events.

Der Blick über die Innenstadt zeigt im Vordergrund das Geschäfts- und Freizeitzentrum Bleicherufer, das seine Herkunft als ehemaliges Schlachthofgelände nicht mehr erkennen lässt. Der an einen Schiffsbug erinnernde Hauptbau ist eine erste Hoteladresse.

The view of the inner city shows the business and leisure centre Bleicherufer - not even the slightest trace is left of its original function as an abattoir. The main building has the shape of a ship's bow and houses a first-class hotel.

Der mächtige Bulle erinnert heute an den früheren Schlachthof am Bleicherufer.

The great bull acts as a reminder of the abattoirs at Bleicherufer.

Ein Stadtteil verändert sein Gesicht. Die Feldstadt als ehemalige Vorstadt ist zu einem attraktiven Wohngebiet und Geschäftsstandort herangewachsen. Dem Abriss des Schlachthofes folgte vor wenigen Jahren der Bau des ersten großen innerstädtischen Geschäfts- und Freizeitzentrums am Bleicherufer in unmittelbarer Nachbarschaft eines ebenfalls neuen Wohngebietes.

A district changes its face. Feldstadt has become an attractive suburb and business location. After the abattoirs had been demolished a few years prior, the first large innercity centre for both business and leisure was created at Bleicherufer, in the immediate vicinity of a new residential area.

Hightech und Bootsidylle. Das Datenverarbeitungszentrum ist nur von der nordwestlichen Ausfallstraße nach Lübeck vom Lankower See getrennt. - Ein Bürostandort entsteht an der Einfallstraße aus Richtung Wismar. Nur die Bahnstrecke durchschneidet die Nachbarschaft zum Medeweger See.

High-tech and the leisure of boating. The centre for data processing is divided from the north western arterial road to Lübeck by Lankower See. An office block is being developed near the road, leading traffic in from Wismar. Only the railway line runs between the complex and Medeweger See.

In unmittelbarer Nachbarschaft des Ziegelsees bieten die Helios-Kliniken Schwerin moderne Heilbehandlungen für die Schweriner, aber auch über die westmecklenburgische Region hinaus.
Zu den Helios-Kliniken gehört die Carl-Friedrich-Flemming-Nervenklinik, die hier auf dem Sachsenberg bereits 1830 ihrer Bestimmung übergeben wurde.

In close proximity to Ziegelsee, Helios-Kliniken Schwerin offer the people of Schwerin and patients from the region of Western Mecklenburg state-of-the-art medical treatment. Helios-Kliniken include the Carl-Friedrich-Flemming Psychiatric Clinic, which was first opened on Sachsenberg in 1830.

Das „Tor" zur Telekom in Lankow.

The entrance to Telekom in Lankow.

Wasser, die Parkanlagen des Zoos und das Verkehrsgeschehen auf Straße und Schiene am Grünen Tal. Im Vordergrund das Gebäude der AOK.

Water, the zoo and road and rail traffic in the Grünes Tal. In the foreground, the AOK building.

Der Norddeutsche Rundfunk, „das Beste am Norden", hat in Schwerin wohl seinen besten Standort gefunden. Im bewaldeten Bereich zwischen Schweriner See und Faulem See ist das Landesfunkhaus des NDR vor wenigen Jahren errichtet worden.
Beide Seen begrenzen auch die Parkanlage des Schweriner Zoos mit seinem vielfältigen einheimischen und exotischen Tierbestand.

The north German radio station "das Beste am Norden" (the north at its best) has found its place in Schwerin. In the wooded area of Schweriner See and Fauler See, the state radio station of the NDR was established a few years ago.
The lakes also border on the park area of Schwerin's zoo, which is home to a great variety of local and exotic animals.

Blick über den Zoo und das nahe Strandbad in Zippendorf.

View across the zoo and bathing in Zippendorf.

Bei klarer Luft ermöglicht der Fernsehturm die Sicht bis zu den Türmen von Wismar und bis zur Ostsee. Vom Restaurant und vom Rundgang in 100 Meter Höhe bietet sich ein einmaliger Blick auf die Stadt und über den Schweriner See.

On a clear day the television tower affords a view as far as the towers of Wismar and the Baltic Sea. The restaurant and the outlook at a heigth of 100 metres afford a unique view of the city and Schweriner See.

Zippendorfer Strand und Zippendorf am Südufer des Schweriner Sees.

It takes only a few minutes to get to the promenade of Zippendorf at Schweriner See.

Baden und Surfen ist nicht nur wie hier am Zippendorfer Strand sondern an vielen Ufern der städtischen Seen möglich.

Zippendorfer Strand and many other lakes around Schwerin attract many visitors interested in bathing and surfing.

Die neu gestaltete Uferpromenade mit ihrem Strandleben, den freizeitsportlichen Möglichkeiten zu Wasser und zu Lande und mit einem reichhaltigen kulturellen Angebot ist gut erreichbar vom Stadtzentrum mit dem Dampfer, zu Fuß oder per Rad am bewaldeten Seeufer entlang oder auch per Auto oder Straßenbahn.

The newly developed promenade on the lake offers an array of leisure and cultural possibilities. It can be easily reached from the city, using the steamer, on foot or by bicycle along the wooded path of the lake, or by car or tram.

Zu Wasser und zu Lande bietet der Schweriner See alle Möglichkeiten für Freizeit und Erholung.

Schweriner See, ideal for weekend outings, sport and leisure time.

Beschauliche Ruhe auf der Marstallhalbinsel bereits in unmittelbarer Nachbarschaft zur Innenstadt.

Peace and tranquility on Marstallhalbinsel, close to the city.

Kanäle verbinden die Seen wie hier zwischen Heidensee und Ziegelsee...

The lakes are connected by a canal system, as between Heidensee and Ziegelsee...

… und zwischen Ziegelsee und Schweriner See.

… and between Ziegelsee and Schweriner See.

Am Ostorfer See zwischen Görries und Neumühle. Vom höchsten Punkt der Stadt grüßt der Neumühler Wasserturm die Reisenden schon von weit her.

Ostorfer See between Görries and Neumühle. From the highest point of the city, the Neumühler Wasserturm greets visitors from afar.

Bootssteg am Neumühler See. Der sechs Kilometer lange Rinnensee im Nordwesten der Stadt bietet an seinen Ufern ein Wandergebiet von besonderer Schönheit mit seinen Buchenbeständen auf den Steilhängen und dem urwüchsigen Quellgebiet des Friedrichsthaler Forstes.

Jetty at Neumühler See. The six kilometre long lake in the northwest of the city invites visitors to enjoy the extraordinary beauty of the steep slopes covered with beech trees, and the unspoiled headwaters of Friedrichsthaler Forst.

Die Insel Kaninchenwerder im Schweriner See ist beliebter Ausflugsort. Eine Schiffslinie ermöglicht nicht nur Bootsbesitzern den Besuch der Insel, die zu Spaziergängen und zum Rundblick vom Turm auf dem Jesarberg einlädt.

The island of Kaninchenwerder in Schweriner See is a popular destination for outings. A steamer takes visitors to the island. The island's tower has been built on Jesarberg and affords a lovely panoramic view.

Nirgendwo ist die hüglige Endmoränenlandschaft Schwerins so offensichtlich wie am Lankower See zwischen Weststadt, Lankow und Neumühle.

At Lankower See between Weststadt, Lankow and Neumühle, the hilly terminal moraine landscape is most evident.

Eine der typischen Endmoränenlandschaften in und um Schwerin. Die Eiszeit hinterließ nicht nur Seen, hügliges Gelände und große Findlinge sondern auch viele eiszeitliche Restlöcher, wie hier an der bewaldeten Uferzone des Schweriner Sees.

A typical terminal moraine is part of the cityscape of Schwerin. Not only did the Ice Age leave behind lakes, hilly areas and large boulders but also many indentations, as shown here on the wooded slopes of Schweriner See.

In der Ferne zieht sich das blaue Band des Schweriner Sees durch die hüglige Endmoränenlandschaft mit ihren gelben Rapsfeldern und grünen Wiesen.
Das ehemalige Dorf Warnitz und die neue Wohnsiedlung Friedrichsthal im städtischen Landschaftsgürtel.

In the distance Schweriner See winds its way through the hilly terminal moraine shelf like a blue ribbon through green meadows and fields of rape.
The former village of Warnitz and the new residential area of Friedrichsthal as part of the urban green belt.

Landschaft und Stadt stehen auch dort im Dialog, wo in den letzten Jahrzehnten große Wohnsiedlungen entstanden wie hier in Lankow zwischen Lankower See und Medeweger See.

Landscape and city form a complete unit where large residential areas were created as in Lankow between Lankower See and Medeweger See.

Der Blick von Norden über den Ziegelsee zeigt beeindruckend die Silhoutte der Stadt.

The view from the north across Ziegelsee shows the impressive skyline of the city.

Der Aubach speist den innerstädtischen Pfaffenteich. Er durchfließt die nördlich gelegenen Seen und bietet mit ihnen reizvolle Wanderstrecken im Aubachtal.

Aubach feeds into Pfaffenteich and makes its way through the northern lakes. The Aubachtal, a valley, offers charming trails for hikers.